PARAGUAY

...in Pictures

Courtesy of Inter-American Development Bank

PARAGUAY

...in Pictures

Prepared by
Nathan A. Haverstock

Lerner Publications Company
Minneapolis

Courtesy of Inter-American Development Bank

A worker feeds chickens on a farm about 15 miles east of Asunción.

This book is an all-new edition in the Visual Geography Series. Previous editions were published by Sterling Publishing Company, New York City. The text, set in 10/12 Century Textbook, is fully revised and updated, and new photographs, maps, charts, and captions have been added.

LIBRARY OF CONGRESS CATALOGING-IN-PUBLICATION DATA

Haverstock, Nathan A.
    Paraguay in pictures.

    (Visual geography series)
    Includes index.
    Summary: Text and photographs examine the land, history, government, people, and economy of this small landlocked republic in the heart of South America.
    1. Paraguay. [1. Paraguay] I. Title. II. Series: Visual geography series (Minneapolis, Minn.)
    F2668.H38   1987   989.2   87-3659
    ISBN 0-8225-1819-8 (lib. bdg.)

International Standard Book Number: 0-8225-1819-8
Library of Congress Catalog Card Number: 87-3659

VISUAL GEOGRAPHY SERIES®

Publisher
Harry Jonas Lerner
Associate Publisher
Nancy M. Campbell
Executive Series Editor
Mary M. Rodgers
Editorial Assistant
Nora W. Kniskern
Illustrations Editors
Nathan A. Haverstock
Karen A. Sirvaitis
Consultants/Contributors
Dr. Ruth F. Hale
Nathan A. Haverstock
Sandra K. Davis
Designer
Jim Simondet
Cartographer
Carol F. Barrett
Indexer
Kristine S. Schubert
Production Manager
Gary J. Hansen

Courtesy of Mike R. Rassier

During his free time this youth rides a trail bike down Paraguay's dirt roads.

Acknowledgments

Title page photo courtesy of Mike R. Rassier.

Elevation contours adapted from *The Times Atlas of the World*, seventh comprehensive edition (New York: Times Books, 1985).

4 5 6 7 8 9 10 – JR – 01 00 99 98 97 96 95

Students at the Caazapá agricultural school, where the children of farmers learn to carry on their fathers' profession, discuss a crop of strawberries with their instructor.

Contents

PARAGUAY

N

Department Boundaries

0   100 Miles
0   100 Kilometers

BOLIVIA

CHACO

NUEVA ASUNCION

ALTO PARAGUAY

PRESIDENTE HAYES

BOQUERON

Filadelfia

AMAMBAY

CONCEPCION

Cerro
Corá

Pedro Juan Caballero

BRAZIL

Aquidaban R.

Concepción

Ypané R.

Verde R.

Montelindo R.

Trans-Chaco Highway

Jejui-Guazu R.

CANENDIYU

Paraguay R.

SAN PEDRO

Pilcomayo R.

ALTO
PARANA

CAAGUAZU

Acaray R.

CORDILLERA

Lake Ypacarai

Coronel Oviedo

ITAIPU DAM

ARGENTINA

ASUNCION

Yaguarón

CENTRAL

GUAIRA

Ciudad
del Este

Iguacu R.

IGUACU FALLS

Ybycui

Villarrica

CAAZAPA

PARAGUARI

Central Paraguayan RR

Tebicuary R.

Santa
Catalina

Pan-American Hwy.

ITAPUA

Alto Parana R.

NEEMBUCU

MISIONES

Trinidad

Encarnación

Yacíretá

Posadas

PARAGUAY

SOUTH AMERICA

0   1000 Miles
0   1000 Kilometers

EQUATOR

80°   60°   40°

PACIFIC
OCEAN

0°

20°

40°

ATLANTIC
OCEAN

METRIC CONVERSION CHART
To Find Approximate Equivalents

WHEN YOU KNOW:	MULTIPLY BY:	TO FIND:
AREA		
acres	0.41	hectares
square miles	2.59	square kilometers
CAPACITY		
gallons	3.79	liters
LENGTH		
feet	30.48	centimeters
yards	0.91	meters
miles	1.61	kilometers
MASS (weight)		
pounds	0.45	kilograms
tons	0.91	metric tons
VOLUME		
cubic yards	0.77	cubic meters
TEMPERATURE		
degrees Fahrenheit	0.56 (*after* subtracting 32)	degrees Celsius

The Acaray Dam, built in the early 1960s near the junction of the Acaray and Paraná rivers, was Paraguay's first source of hydroelectric energy. It now supplies all of the power requirements of the capital city of Asunción.

Introduction

Like other Latin American countries, Paraguay is a poor country whose economy is based largely on agriculture. Nevertheless, the nation differs from other Spanish-American countries in language, in culture, and in history. Most Paraguayans are bilingual, speaking not only Spanish but also Guarani—the tongue of Paraguay's original Indian inhabitants.

The Guarani tongue survives in Paraguay as an official language largely because of the nation's early settlement by the Jesuits—learned Catholic missionaries with a cultural understanding well in advance of their day. During more than a century and a half—until their expulsion in 1767—the Jesuits achieved a notable example of communal living for themselves and the Indians. Through a network of missionary settlements 150,000 Guarani lived and worked together with these missionaries from Spain, who converted the Indians to Christianity.

The Jesuits were not the last religious group to settle in Paraguay. At the turn of the twentieth century, Mennonites living in Canada and the United States sought out the isolation of Paraguay to escape the scorn and intimidation they had been subjected to in some areas of the northern lands. In Paraguay the hardworking Mennonites practiced their communal faith freely and established farming settlements both in the east and in the wilderness lands of the inhospitable Gran Chaco. Some of their descendants—the

7

Cattle raising is a major industry in Paraguay. These gauchos (cowboys) are leaving an estancia (ranch) in western Paraguay on their way to the open range.

largest foreign ethnic group in the Paraguayan population—still occupy the Chaco region and worship at a simple, whitewashed church in Filadelfia (Spanish for Philadelphia—the city of brotherly love).

To preserve order in their remote land, Paraguayans have allowed caudillos (military dictators) to rule their country since 1811, when they gained independence from Spain. Only twice in the history of the nation has there been a presidential election with more than one candidate on the ballot. One nineteenth-century caudillo—Francisco Solano López—led Paraguay into a disastrous war against Uruguay and two much more powerful neighbors, Argentina and Brazil. By the time the war was over Paraguay's population had been reduced by more than half.

Other caudillos—anxious to go down in history as builders, not destroyers—have done more to improve the country. Such a leader was General Alfredo Stroessner, who ruled Paraguay from 1954 until his overthrow in 1989. Elected—largely without opposition—to five-year terms of office eight times, Stroessner governed

German-speaking Mennonites, who emigrated from Germany and the United States during the early twentieth century, worship at simple, whitewashed churches such as this one in Filadelfia.

Paraguay longer than any of his predecessors. To help maintain his rule, Stroessner brutally crushed dissent, concentrating his efforts on building the nation's economy rather than on improving social justice. Yet rivalries within Stroessner's own political party led to a violent coup in February 1989, when General Andrés Rodríguez seized power. Once a close ally of Stroessner's, Rodríguez relaxed media censorship and allowed opposition parties to participate in elections. Paraguay held the first free elections in its history in 1993, when Juan Carlos Wasmosy became the new civilian president.

While most Paraguayans have lived with poor education, health care, and housing, government funds have gone primarily to improve Paraguay's transportation and energy systems. For example, large sums have been expended to build an international airport. A newly constructed city—Ciudad del Este—provides a direct land route to the Brazilian port of Paranaguá.

By far the grandest undertaking of Stroessner's long administration was the construction of a series of hydroelectric dams to harness the power of the Alto Paraná River. With the completion of the first dam in the 1960s, Paraguay not only satisfied its own power needs but also became an exporter of surplus power to Argentina, Paraguay's partner in the construction. The Itaipu Dam—built jointly with Brazil and completed in 1981—is the world's largest single source of hydroelectric energy. Despite the success of other hydroelectric projects completed in the late 1980s, Paraguay still suffers from rising prices and a weak economy.

In a fuel-short nation, makeshift passenger vehicles—like this taxi at Encarnación, near the Argentine border—still exist.

Courtesy of Inter-American Development Bank

Blessed with several navigable rivers, Paraguay relies heavily on its waterways for commercial transport, since its roads are often impassable.

1) The Land

The Republic of Paraguay is a landlocked country of southern South America long off the beaten track of world commerce. Bounded on three sides—the west, the south, and the southeast—by Argentina, Paraguay shares much of its long eastern border with Brazil and its northern border with Bolivia. With an area of 157,043 square miles, Paraguay is slightly smaller than the state of California.

Rivers are the lifeblood of Paraguay. Before the air age they were the only means of communication with the world beyond the oceans. Today those rivers supply Paraguay not only with all the electricity it needs but also with surplus power, which the nation sells to its South American neighbors to double its gross national product.

Rivers

Most of Paraguay's population lives clustered along the banks of the Paraguay River. Women wash their clothes in its silt-laden waters, and farmers divert the river's flow to irrigate their fields. Producers of meat, timber, cotton, tobacco, and other crops rely on riverboats to carry their commerce into world markets. The whistling of river craft—a typical but also particularly important sound in Paraguay—signals the arrival and departure of people and products.

Paraguay occupies a large part of the basin of the Paraguay River, which flows south across the country after defining a part of Paraguay's border with Brazil. The river divides the country into two sharply contrasting regions. The western section is known as the Gran Chaco—a 95,350-square-mile, sparsely inhabited tract of scrub forests and savanna (grassland). Eastern Paraguay is a 61,693-square-mile area containing the majority of the population and the most fertile land. The Verde and Montelindo rivers flow from the Gran Chaco into the Paraguay River, and the Aquidaban, Ypané, Jejui Guazú, and Tebicuary rivers water eastern Paraguay.

The Paraguay River flows into the Alto (upper) Paraná, broadening this mighty waterway as it moves the final 800 miles into the Río de la Plata and out into the Atlantic Ocean between Argentina and Uruguay. To the south and east the Alto Paraná marks the boundary between Paraguay and Brazil and between Paraguay and northern Argentina. From the west,

Courtesy of Mike R. Rassier

After the cotton is picked, it will be transported to market by riverboat.

the Pilcomayo River traces Paraguay's southwestern border with Argentina before flowing into the Paraguay River at Asunción, the Paraguayan capital.

Courtesy of Inter-American Development Bank

A river has been diverted to power this hydroelectric dam (center left).

Paraguay occupies substantial portions of both the Pilcomayo and Alto Paraná river basins, which encompass farmlands that are important for the future development of the country. If the centuries-old dream of developing these rivers into a single great inland waterway were ever realized, Paraguay would have a strategic location. Similarly, if the Alto Paraná Basin were linked to the Amazon Basin, the immense interior of the South American continent would be opened up.

During times of flooding Paraguay's broad rivers feature floating islands of matted plants, such as water hyacinths. These islets are covered with flowers of many hues and figure in the history and legends of the country.

Topography and Climate

In the eastern third of Paraguay lies part of the huge Paraná Plateau, with elevations rising up to about 1,000 feet. The plateau extends into Paraguay from southern Brazil and becomes a steep slope that is topped by cliffs of impressive height. The Alto Paraná River cuts a deep trench through the plateau. Nearby, along the border between Brazil and Argentina, the Iguaçu River foams over a high ledge at Iguaçu to form a great waterfall before joining the Alto Paraná. Visible from Paraguay, Iguaçu Falls substantially exceed Niagara Falls in height, size, and volume of water.

Two hilly ridges extend to the west from the Paraná Plateau. One of them approaches the northern city of Concepción, and the other reaches the capital, Asunción. Most Paraguayans live along the highland from Asunción to Encarnación, in the southeastern part of the country. The rest of Paraguay is mostly lowlands, some of which are flooded annually by one or another river. An important lowland lies in the heart of the country, southeast of Con-

Independent Picture Service

Visible from Paraguay, Iguaçu Falls lie on the border between Argentina and Brazil and are the most spectacular falls in South America. Named after the Guarani word for great waters, Iguaçu Falls are about 2.5 miles wide with more than 20 separate cascades (only one is shown above) **that average 200 feet in height. Above the falls, a cloud of mist nearly 100 feet high mixes with the sunlight to create colorful rainbows.**

Independent Picture Service

Gradually, Paraguayan pioneers are converting the Chaco wilderness into cultivated fields.

When the Trans-Chaco Highway was built, numerous stone and cement arches were constructed to bridge swampy lowland areas.

cepción, and another—a triangle-shaped region—is situated south of Asunción.

The Gran Chaco occupies the entire western half of the country between the Paraguay River and the Bolivian border. An alluvial plain, the Chaco was formed when alluvium—silt, sand, clay, gravel, or similar loose sediment—was deposited across the region by flowing water. This sparsely inhabited wilderness is swampy during the rainy season and parched during the dry season. Recently a road was built through the Chaco, which has encouraged pioneers to settle in the region.

While northern Paraguay along the Bolivian border is located within the tropics, the remainder of the country is subtropical, similar in some respects to the state of Florida. Although winter (April to September) is somewhat cooler than summer (October to March), Paraguay's climate is warm and mild. Winter temperatures are in the sixties and seventies, with an average of 63° F.

In the summer the thermometer ranges from the high seventies to the nineties, with an average of 83° F and occasional highs of 110° F. At all times of the year temperatures are exceedingly variable. Cold fronts alternate quickly with warm ones, sometimes causing a temperature change as sharp as 30° F in half an hour. The cold air masses move up from as far south as the Antarctic regions, and the warm air masses originate in the equatorial Amazon.

Rain falls most heavily on the Paraná Plateau and lessens toward the west. Generally speaking, however, Paraguay's rainfall is abundant. Asunción averages about 50 inches of rain per year. The only relatively arid region is in the northwestern corner of the Gran Chaco.

A native of Paraguay, the carnauba palm is found on marshlands near the Paraguay River. The tree has an edible root and yields a hard brownish wax used in polishes for floors, furniture, and shoes.

13

Vegetation

Paraguay's vegetation—like its rainfall—is most dense in the east, where semideciduous forests (whose trees lose only some of their leaves each year) cover the hilly upland. Tall, broadleafed trees, some of them evergreen, are thickest in the moist valleys of the plateau. Between the plateau and the Paraguay River, open savanna, with coarse grass and patches of palms, extends across the land. Scrub woodlands are found toward the east. A species of holly whose leaves provide Paraguay's national beverage, yerba maté (holly tea), grows wild in the eastern region.

In the distinctive Gran Chaco, leaf-shedding scrub woodlands thrive, yielding the commercially valuable quebracho—a hardwood from which tannin, a substance used in tanning leather, is extracted. Toward the west, as rainfall decreases and thorn bushes and brush become more common,

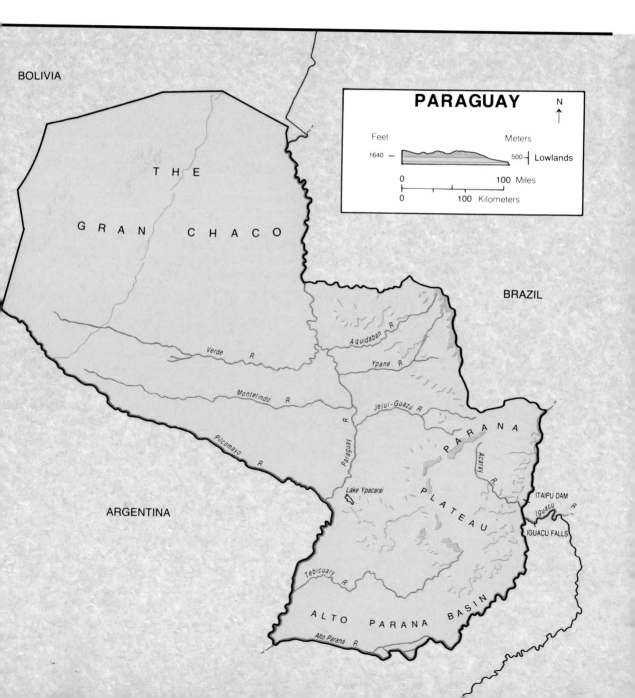

Courtesy of David Mangurian

The vegetation of Paraguay is rich and varied, with some species of ancient origin and others that are found almost nowhere else in the world. Plant life ranges from brilliantly colored flowers and commercially valuable forest products to parasitical growths, such as those clinging to the tree below.

Photo by Don Irish

there are open areas of grassy savanna. During the dry season, patches of alkali (salty soil) and small saltwater ponds appear in these open areas.

Wildlife

In the largely unsettled and unspoiled land of Paraguay, wildlife abounds. Jaguars, ocelots (medium-sized wildcats), deer, peccaries (wild pigs), anteaters, capybaras (tailless, aquatic, South American rodents), tapirs, and other mammals roam the Chaco. The wide range of animals gave the Chaco its name, which is derived from the Quechua Indian word *chacu*, which means "an abundance of animal life." Reptiles include poisonous coral snakes and semi-aquatic anacondas, which sometimes reach 30 feet in length.

The country's bird life is similarly varied. Kingfishers, bitterns, snowy egrets, storks, Muscovy ducks, pheasants, quail, rheas (South American ostriches), and partridges are a few of the species commonly found.

In the warm, humid climate of Paraguay, numerous insects bother both man and domesticated animals. Malaria-carrying anopheles mosquitoes constantly threaten Paraguayans. Gnats are also on hand to cause skin irritations and infection. Fly larvae and several varieties of ticks bury themselves under the skin of humans and animals, resulting in sores and swellings. The pique, a small, louse-like parasite, can bore into the tough soles of feet. Farmers must contend with insect pests, including leaf-cutting ants and boll weevils, which can cause severe crop losses.

Independent Picture Service

The largest South American land mammal, the tapir is a hoofed animal related to the horse and rhinoceros. Tapirs use their flexible snouts to forage for food at night amid dense foliage, feeding on twigs, leaves, and fruit. Because tapirs are nonaggressive, they hide in water or dense forest when danger is near.

The capybara, the largest living rodent, grows to about four feet long and can weigh up to 100 pounds. Although they run clumsily because of partially webbed feet, capybaras swim well and can remain underwater for several minutes. They live in pairs or families along the banks of Paraguay's rivers and lakes.

Insects thrive in Paraguay's warm, humid climate. Here, ranchers treat a calf infected by blowfly—a relative of the housefly that lays eggs in the flesh of cattle, causing damage and sometimes death.

Life thrives in Paraguay's many rivers, especially in the Paraguay River. Commercially important fish include freshwater salmon and the dorado, a coveted game fish. Catfish also are numerous. Among the fish strangest to people from other parts of the world are lungfish, which seal themselves in mud during the dry season, and bloodthirsty piranhas, which, though small, travel in large schools and can reduce a deer to a skeleton in a matter of minutes.

Mineral Resources

In contrast to its abundant wildlife, Paraguay has few known natural resources. The country's soil is generally deficient in mineral nutrients—a deficiency that afflicts both livestock and humans. Though there are repeated rumors that oil has been discovered in the Gran Chaco, they have never been proven. The only fuel found in the country is peat—a compact, organic material formed by decaying vegetation that represents the first stage in the transition to coal.

Paraguay has some commercially exploitable deposits of sandstone and limestone.

17

Virtually all of Paraguay's soil contains clay, which gives the earth its reddish hue. Many towns have capitalized on this resource by building small facilities to manufacture bricks and tiles from local materials.

Clay prized in the manufacture of brick and tile is found almost everywhere. Extensive, potentially valuable deposits of marble and serpentine (a mineral used in industry as a source of magnesium and in architecture as a decorative stone) are known to exist. Paraguay also has manganese and copper reserves, as well as small deposits of high-grade iron ore, but none of these has been mined recently.

Asunción

Since the founding of Asunción in 1537—less than half a century after Columbus discovered the New World—the city has remained an important center of government. Besides being the government seat and the country's most important commercial city, Asunción serves as the hub for a semicircular area extending about 60 miles from the city itself—an area that is sometimes called "Greater Asunción."

The Paraguayan capital rises from the banks of the Paraguay River up the slopes of a low hill. At the top, a large, modern church called La Encarnación crowns the hill. Approaching the city by river steamer, one observes the bustling activity of

Travelers await a ferryboat that will transport them across the Paraguay River to Asunción.

Downtown Asunción bustles with activity during the work week.

Asunción, with its 729,000 people. The bulk of the country's commerce with the world passes through the old white Customs House, a landmark since colonial days. Along the docks giant cranes load and unload supplies.

From the air the city offers a view of red-tiled roofs, broad streets, green expanses, and patches of bright flowers. Only a few Spanish-Moorish buildings with grilled windows and rooms built around central patios survive from the colonial period. Although the city follows a Spanish design, with rectangular blocks laid out around a central plaza, the plain buildings reflect the fact that Asunción is

Located on Paraguay's border with Brazil, Ciudad del Este (formerly Puerto Presidente Stroessner) thrives upon the flow of goods and people between the two countries.

19

the chief city of a comparatively poor country.

But the capital is not devoid of ornamental structures. Patterned after the Louvre in Paris, the Government Palace was built during the disastrous War of the Triple Alliance (1865-1873), and the Pantheon of Heroes—built about the same time—copies Les Invalides, also in Paris. In addition, a number of attractive parks grace the city, some of them occupying the grounds of beautiful estates.

Secondary Cities

While Asunción is the nation's only large city, there are several smaller communities of considerable interest. About 200 miles to the north on the Paraguay River is Concepción, which has a population of 26,000. Increasing commerce with Brazil—including trade in cattle, hides, lumber, quebracho, tobacco, and yerba mate—passes through the town.

Concepción's commerce has had a rippling effect, enhancing the vitality of Pedro Juan Caballero. With a population of 80,000, Pedro Juan Caballero is located some 200 miles northeast of Concepción on the Brazilian border. A similar distance from Asunción to the east is Villarrica, population 22,000. Centrally located in eastern Paraguay and boasting a colonial cathedral, Villarrica is a marketing hub for cotton, tobacco, sugar, yerba mate, hides, meat, and domestic wines.

East of Villarrica along the Alto Paraná River, Ciudad del Este (formerly Puerto Presidente Stroessner) was recently built to accommodate those involved in the construction of the Itaipu Dam. Until the dam's completion in 1981, this was the fastest growing city in Paraguay, reaching a population of 110,000.

South of Ciudad del Este, also on the Alto Paraná River and across from the Argentine city of Posadas, is Encarnación, with a population of about 31,000. Rebuilt after its destruction by a tornado in 1926, Encarnación is one of Paraguay's most modern towns. At the end of the Central Paraguayan Railroad, Encarnación is an active river port, from which good roads lead northeast to Iguaçu Falls and northwest to Asunción. Trains are transported by ferryboat across the Alto Paraná River at Encarnación to continue on to Buenos Aires, the Argentine capital.

Eroded hillsides, makeshift housing, and rubbish are typical of the slum areas of the capital city.

Asunción's port and commercial section have long been vital to the Paraguayan capital, whose main link with the outside world is the commerce of the Paraguay River.

At Ciudad del Este, the Amistad (friendship) Bridge spans the Alto Paraná River to link Paraguay with Brazil. The bridge is nearly a third of a mile long.

One of the most outstanding examples of architecture from the Jesuit missions is the church at Trinidad. Designed by Juan Primoli, an architect from Milan, Italy, the church was built under his supervision by the Guarani craftspeople during the mid-eighteenth century. High-relief carvings adorn the main facade as well as the doorway, which is flanked by ornate columns. The church has recently been restored, and a museum has been established to preserve Jesuit relics.

Courtesy of Edith Lurvey

2) History and Government

Paraguay's history has been marked by long periods of peace that occasionally have been interrupted by the destruction of war. The nation's people have endured the excesses of both homegrown tyrants and foreign foes. Paraguayans have been plagued with poverty, and they have been dominated by foreign interests—mainly Spanish, Argentine, and Brazilian. In a broader sense, this means that much of Paraguay's history has been determined by the unwinding of events elsewhere—events that Paraguay has been powerless to shape. Only in very recent years has Paraguay begun to fashion its own destiny as a nation by focusing on its internal development.

Founding of Asunción

Spanish settlers established the first successful colony in the Río de la Plata area

Courtesy of Edith Lurvey

An angel carved from stone at Trinidad reveals the Guarani influence on religious themes.

and the territories that today form the nations of Bolivia and Uruguay.

The Jesuit Settlements

In 1588 members of the Roman Catholic Society of Jesus, known as the Jesuits, arrived in Paraguay. As elsewhere in Spain's New World dominions, the mission of this religious order was twofold—to bring Christianity to the native inhabitants and to provide for their education and welfare. Of the several groups of missionaries in the area, the Jesuits soon became the most important.

By the late sixteenth century, the Jesuits had succeeded in gathering the 150,000 Guarani Indians living in the territory of Paraguay into agricultural colonies, or *reducciones*. Within these settlements, the

at Asunción in 1537. Two factors determined the location of the settlement—its nearness to the Paraguay River and its setting in an attractive and pleasant valley with readily accessible farmland.

Asunción flourished. Within 20 years of its founding 1,500 Spanish families had settled there, had built a cathedral and a textile mill, and had begun to raise cattle. For nearly two centuries Asunción continued to be the most important center of Spanish power within the area of the Río de la Plata Basin.

From Asunción expeditions set out to explore, colonize, and exploit the land and resources of much of southern South America. As the region's most important commercial town, Asunción played a central role in the development of the Spanish Empire. Expeditions outfitted in the city settled northern and western Argentina

Independent Picture Service

A colonial facade influenced by Spanish architectural styles graces the Church of San Francisco in the capital city of Asunción.

Guarani were introduced to European civilization and religion. Versatile and dedicated teachers, the Jesuits taught their wards improved methods of farming and livestock raising. The Jesuits also tried to protect the Indians from Brazil-based slave hunters. These hunters frequently came into Paraguayan territory to round up Indians, whom they sold elsewhere on the continent.

For their part, the Indians of Paraguay proved to be good pupils. But the Jesuits also kept the strong Guarani culture alive while overlaying it with imported Spanish ways and religious practices. To this day the Guarani language continues to be the most widely spoken tongue of Paraguay. For their selfless and remarkably successful efforts in Paraguay, the Jesuits won worldwide acclaim as extenders of Western ways. The Jesuit reducciones were studied in universities as models of religious practice combined with communal living.

In addition to working in the fields, the Guarani built churches and cathedrals, carved images of the saints, and painted

An intricately carved doorway ornaments the entrance to a Jesuit mission.

murals and retablos—panels adorned with religious scenes and symbols. They learned to play the guitar and the harp, and they sang religious and love songs in their native tongue.

The success of the Jesuits led to their undoing. The Spanish crown and its bu-

All that remains of this mission, established in the sixteenth century by the Jesuits, is the ruin of an arcade (covered passageway) completed shortly before the missionaries were expelled from Paraguay in 1767.

Though never completed, this colonial church reveals basic architectural elements.

reaucracy became envious of the Jesuit-run settlements. There were fears that the Jesuits were becoming too powerful in the affairs of Paraguay, and in 1767 the king of Spain officially expelled the Jesuits from the Spanish colonies in Paraguay and elsewhere in the New World.

Unfortunately, the Jesuits were not replaced by any effective system. Stripped of their leadership, the reducciones fell into a state of disrepair. Many of the Indians dispersed, and, although for the most part they remained converts to Christianity, they practiced the religion in their own fashion.

Neglect by Imperial Spain

Paraguay—once prosperous and admired by many Europeans as an isolated paradise —entered a period of imperial neglect. Eventually, officials in Spain drew up plans to tighten the administration of its empire, which had grown too large for highly centralized control.

In 1776 the Spanish monarchs made Paraguay a province within the newly established Viceroyalty of La Plata. This powerful state had its capital in Buenos Aires. Paraguayans resented their new subordinate status. They could do little more than grumble about it, however, since Buenos Aires controlled the mouth of the Paraná River and its access to world markets—the lifeline of Paraguay. In the late eighteenth and early nineteenth centuries, Paraguay was completely neglected by its Spanish rulers, who were involved in Europe's Napoleonic Wars.

José Gaspar Rodríguez de Francia

In 1811 Paraguay became the first area in the Spanish New World to declare and maintain its independence. In making their declaration, the country's leaders, dominated by José Gaspar Rodríguez de Francia, were careful to declare their independence from Buenos Aires as well as from Spain.

25

Simon Bolívar's role as the liberator of South America is commemorated by this monument in front of the Legislative Palace in Asunción. A South American soldier and statesman, Bolívar was instrumental in establishing freedom for most of the Spanish colonies on the continent. Born in Venezuela, Bolívar gained independence for his homeland in 1817 and went on to free Colombia, Ecuador, Peru, and Bolivia. Although Paraguay was able to gain independence on its own — perhaps because Spain had largely ignored the remote region — its freedom hinged on that of the surrounding New World colonies.

Photo by Don Irish

Francia stepped into the leadership of the new nation almost by default. A student of history and theology, he was considered the country's most highly educated man. Austere, frugal, and harsh, he also suffered from epilepsy and depression. Despite these physical and psychological difficulties, Francia ruled Paraguay as a dictator without interruption from 1811 until his death in 1840.

Francia's antiforeign, antichurch policies aimed to benefit the disadvantaged classes of society — Indians and mestizos (those of mixed Indian-and-Spanish bloodlines). Except for the few concerns that he controlled personally, Francia cut off all trade and contacts with the outside world. He dissolved the monasteries in Paraguay and excluded the Roman Catholic church from any role in the country, including local church affairs. Having abandoned these contacts, Francia depended on the army, the police, and innumerable informers and spies for support.

Francia divided up the country into military districts, then let the efficient and disciplined army control the countryside while the police were given charge of the towns. He repressed all who might or who actually did oppose him — all those of pure Spanish descent, all who in any way distinguished themselves, all members of what might have been called an upper class. He forced the Indians and mestizos to work for the government as farmers, ranchers, and road builders.

Because Francia aimed to make Paraguay entirely self-sufficient, he introduced improved agricultural technology and developed local industries to eliminate the need for imports and contacts with the outside world. Moreover, no one was allowed to leave the country. For example, when José Gervasio Artigas, the liberator of Uruguay, took refuge in Paraguay, he was forced to remain there until his death. Francia governed the country single-handedly — the entire government bureaucracy consisted of only four clerks and a military force.

Because Francia had not set up any systems for continuing the government—no constitution, no congress, and no political institutions—disorder followed his death in 1840. Having stripped the people of all initiative, he left them with neither the resources nor the skills necessary for self-government. But Francia left as his legacy a unified people with a strong national pride and an economy adequate to the minimum needs of an underdeveloped country.

Carlos Antonio López

The man who emerged as Francia's successor was his nephew, Carol Antonio López, a wealthy rancher. López governed initially as one of two consuls, then as

Paraguayan dictator José Gaspar Rodríguez de Francia styled himself as *El Supremo,* or the Supreme One. Although Francia did much to unify the nation and to increase its industrial and agricultural output, he severely oppressed political freedom. Nevertheless, he was revered by his people, who exalted him as *El Difunto*, or the Deceased One, after his death.

Photo by Organization of American States

president, surrounded by advisers who helped him to administer a system of laws he himself had devised.

Reversing most of Francia's policies, López reopened Paraguayan ports, restored power to the church, and guaranteed the security of property owned by those of pure Spanish descent. He administered his government well enough to win the support of most of the politically influential elements of the country. In 1844 López was elected president, and he ruled as a dictator until his death in 1862.

A progressive, López promoted education. He also helped the church in a material sense by using government funds to build churches, but he strictly subjected the church to the authority of the state. Among his other accomplishments, López abolished slavery, established a newspaper, promoted trade, built a railway, bridged rivers, opened up the Paraguay River to steam navigation, developed the nation's road system, and introduced modern agricultural techniques. Diplomatically, López was both shrewd and successful. He maneuvered between Brazil and Argentina, playing one off against the other, and thus kept the Paraguay and Paraná rivers as free and open to navigation as possible.

Independent Picture Service

Carlos Antonio López, Francia's successor, exercised complete authority from 1841 until 1862, organizing the country along progressive lines.

Though López was as dictatorial as Francia, López's policies suited the times and slightly improved conditions in Paraguay. When López died, Paraguay was a fairly

Independent Picture Service

Located in Asunción's Plaza Constitución, the Legislative Palace — where the Paraguayan congress meets — dates from the time of Carlos Antonio López.

Francisco Solano López, who had been groomed for the presidency by his father, became dictator of Paraguay in 1862 and nearly led the country to destruction in the War of the Triple Alliance.

Francisco Solano López and the War of the Triple Alliance

The third of Paraguay's dictators, López's son, Francisco Solano López—who had been groomed for the presidency almost from birth—was elected president after his father's death. Appointed commander in chief of the army at age 19, he regarded himself as a military genius, equal to Napoleon Bonaparte.

The young López became minister of war and the head of the navy in his father's government. In that post López acquired considerable diplomatic experience and prestige, serving as a diplomatic representative in Europe and successfully mediating a dispute between the provinces of Argentina and Buenos Aires, the Argentine capital. Occasional threats of an outbreak of hostilities against Argentina or Brazil—even against Great Britain or the United States—provided López with a pretext to build up Paraguay's land and naval forces.

When Brazilian troops intervened in a revolution in Uruguay, López declared war on Brazil. In part López feared Brazil was seeking military conquests, but he also was seeking conquests of his own. When Argentina refused to let Paraguayan troops

prosperous nation. It had a constitution, if only on paper, and although the people did not enjoy broad liberties, they did have some material well-being.

Carlos Antonio López began building the Central Paraguayan Railroad in 1854, and Francisco Solano López continued the project. This steam engine was one of the first used when the railroad opened.

Courtesy of Organization of American States

cross Argentine territory to reach southern Brazil, López declared war on Argentina as well. At the end of Uruguay's revolution in 1865, the country joined Brazil and Argentina in a triple alliance against Paraguay. They fought against Paraguay for five years, from 1865 to 1870, when López was killed and Paraguay surrendered.

By the time the destruction was over, Paraguay's population had been reduced from more than 500,000 people to less than half that number. According to the terms of peace, Paraguay lost 55,000 square miles of its territory and was saddled with a huge debt, which the nation was unable to pay off. Some people questioned whether Paraguay would be able to maintain its independence—especially during its six years of occupation by Brazilian and Argentine troops. Indeed, Paraguay's independence was assured only because of the rivalry between Brazilian and Argentine forces.

For 40 years after the War of the Triple Alliance, Paraguay had virtually no military forces—a radical change for a people who historically had spent much of their national treasure for defense. The military uniform became an object of contempt, and Paraguay's standing army consisted of a handful of poorly disciplined draftees.

An Uneasy Freedom

In 1874 General Bernardino Caballero, a war hero, founded the Colorado party and through this conservative group dominated Paraguayan politics for 30 years. During this period Caballero made and unmade presidents at will, hardly affected by the opposing Liberal party.

Despite the disastrous conclusion to the War of the Triple Alliance, Francisco Solano López is revered as one of Paraguay's greatest heroes. This cross marks the spot at Cerro Corá, near the Brazilian border, where López was killed in battle. A national park has been established here to commemorate the fallen leader.

Courtesy of Edith Lurvey

Construction of the Pantheon of Heroes in Asunción was begun during the War of the Triple Alliance but was not completed until 1937. The site now contains the tombs of Carlos Antonio López, Francisco Solano López, two unknown Paraguayan soldiers, and José Félix Estigarribia, a hero of the Chaco War in the 1930s.

In the final months of 1904, however, the Liberals obtained power through a rebellion. To rebuild Paraguay's defense, they created a general staff, started a military school, organized a few military units with modern equipment, and began to enlist men of good character for the nation's armed services. In 1909 compulsory military service was established; in 1912 the army was reorganized, and a serious and sustained effort was made to revitalize it. Foreign military missions helped train the new forces, whose opportunity to prove themselves was not far off.

But the Liberals proved incapable of restoring political stability or of ushering in freedom from revolution. The first eight years of Liberal party rule saw 10 presidents—4 in the year 1911 alone.

Revolutions became a regular part of Paraguay's national life for the next 40 years. Some were purely internal affairs, others the result of foreign intrigues, but none involved major political or economic issues. Almost without exception, the revolutions of this period, up until the end of World War II, resulted from the conflict between personal egos or from political rivalry. Until 1932 presidents served an average of only about two years before being thrown out by rivals.

Paraguayans learned to live with political instability. Despite the turmoil in the capital city, economic development continued in rural areas. Farming and ranching were expanded and modernized, industries were established, and transportation routes were improved. There was steady, if undramatic, progress in health and public education.

Immigrants, encouraged by the government to settle in Paraguay, brought in foreign investment and needed technology and enterprise. In agriculture, Paraguay was soon producing high yields of cotton, tobacco, maize (corn), coffee, sugarcane, manioc (a fleshy root crop), rice, and citrus fruits. The nation also increased its production of valuable forest products such as rubber and yerba mate.

Large corporations also played an important role in settling and developing the land. French, British, and U.S. companies organized the large-scale production of

These Paraguayan cadets were among the first to fly in a nation that in the late 1920s had an air force consisting of just four double-winged planes.

improved breeds of beef cattle and the export of yerba mate and timber. During the years between 1880 and 1915 investment boomed in Paraguay, with foreign financiers and sharp promoters taking over control of the nation's best farmlands and natural resources.

The Chaco War

Both Paraguay and Bolivia had claimed sovereignty over the Chaco since colonial days. Each nation had legal reasons to justify its claim to the area. Under Spain's imperial system, the area was under nominal control of Charcas (present-day Bo-

When the Liberal party came to power in 1904, its members began to rebuild the military, which had been neglected since Paraguay's defeat in the War of the Triple Alliance. These army officers, photographed in 1929, are ready to defend their country against any outside threats.

livia) until late in the eighteenth century, when it was transferred to the authority of Buenos Aires. At that time few cared very much about this bureaucratic action involving an empty piece of wilderness.

In the final years of the nineteenth century, however, new factors came into play that made ownership of the Chaco a matter of intense national pride to both claimants. Humiliated by its defeat in the War of the Triple Alliance, Paraguay saw a chance to restore its national pride by expanding its territory. Bolivia, on the other hand, had lost its access to the Pacific Ocean to Chile in 1884. Access to the Paraguay River would provide Bolivia with a direct route to the Atlantic Ocean via the Río de la Plata.

Title to the now-coveted Chaco became a prime justification for expanding and modernizing the military establishments in both Bolivia and Paraguay. Meddling in the quarrel, Chile urged Bolivia on, while Argentina backed Paraguay. Rumors of vast petroleum deposits located in the disputed area further encouraged hostilities.

In 1928 a Paraguayan attack on a Bolivian outpost touched off a storm of charges and countercharges. The Paraguayan government accused the Standard Oil Company of New Jersey of financing Bolivia's buildup of new arms. Bolivia asserted that Great Britain and Argentina were secretly encouraging Paraguay.

The size and violence of incidents escalated until 1932, when war between the two nations was in full progress. With three times the population of Paraguay, greater wealth, and a German-trained

With the impending threat of the Chaco War, Paraguay's military was expanded further. The cavalry, army, and air force all were modernized.

33

At the turn of the twentieth century, people at the main railroad station in Asunción await trains that will carry them to major destinations in Paraguay.

army, Bolivia was expected to overwhelm its weaker opponent. But Bolivia's government was unstable and corrupt, and Bolivian troops, accustomed to high altitudes, found it difficult to fight in the Chaco's swampy lowlands.

Paraguay, in contrast, had an able president at the time in Eusebio Ayala, and a competent military leader in José Félix Estigarribia. Moreover, Paraguayans genuinely felt that they were defending their homeland. Generally regarded as the aggrieved party, Paraguay enjoyed much private and government sympathy from other nations in the Western Hemisphere, making it easy for Paraguay's government to purchase arms and supplies.

In all about 100,000 troops participated in the Chaco War. During the rainy season men fought in deep mud; during the dry season they often could not find water to drink. Disease took as heavy a toll as actual combat. The war dragged on for three years before hostilities finally came to a halt from sheer exhaustion, and a truce was signed. In 1938 a formal peace treaty confirmed Paraguay's victory and awarded the nation more than 20,000 square miles of land.

A Series of Dictators

After the Chaco War, several of Paraguay's leaders traced their rise to power to the part they had played in the war, a role they often greatly exaggerated. One such hero was General José Félix Estigarribia, who became president on August 15, 1939. Enjoying considerable support in his efforts to reestablish order, the general created yet another dictatorship, which sought the welfare of the people and the strength of the state. Formally embodied in the Constitution of 1940, these ideals were overwhelmingly approved in a vote that represented a show of confidence in Estigarribia.

Under the new authoritarian charter, Paraguay was to be governed by a unicameral (one-house) legislature—composed of a deputy to represent each 25,000 people —and by an advisory council of state. The council included cabinet ministers, the rector of the national university, the Roman Catholic archbishop, and representatives of various industrial, agricultural, financial, and military interests. All Paraguayans over 18 years of age were eligible to vote.

Unfortunately for Paraguay, Estigarribia did not survive to lead his people into the promised new era. Killed in an airplane crash in September 1940, he was succeeded by Higinio Morínigo, a stronger and less humane leader. Morínigo was the second hero of the Chaco War to sit in the presidential chair.

Morínigo immediately began to shape the government to his personal specifications. Less than two months after assuming office, all power was effectively concentrated in his hands, and a one-man rule had begun that was to last eight years. Rejecting democratic and liberal principles, Morínigo presided over the nation as a dictator.

Morínigo's administration imprisoned masses of protesters and instantly crushed attempts at revolt. The coming of World War II, which Morínigo used to make dictatorial rule seem a necessity, lended legitimacy to the regime. The war saw Paraguay's exports of beef, hides, cotton, and quebracho increase greatly in volume and price. United States aid poured in, and both the United States and Brazil financed loans for public works.

Internationally, Morínigo followed the lead of the United States. He broke off relations with the Axis (pro-German) powers in 1942, declared war against them in 1944 —when it was obvious that the Allies (those countries fighting against Germany) would win—and signed the Charter of the United Nations. During the war, however, Morínigo had provided refuge for Axis spies, protected them in their activities, promoted discrimination against Jews, and suppressed demonstrations that supported the Allies.

It was not until 1947 that anyone seriously challenged Morínigo's rule. By the end of the year, an opposing faction of the Colorado party forced Morínigo to leave the country. Elections in early 1948 were won by Juan Natalicio González, who appeared alone on the ballot. After a number of uprisings, the rival faction of the Colorado party, led by Frederíco Chávez, assumed control in 1950. Chávez continued Morínigo's brand of leadership until his overthrow in July 1954. For nearly 35 years after this coup, Paraguay was ruled by a single dictator, General Alfredo Stroessner.

General Alfredo Stroessner ruled Paraguay for over three decades, from 1954 until 1989. Severe restrictions on individual freedom were a hallmark of his dictatorship.

In May 1954 Paraguayan troops paraded through the streets of the capital, just two months before Alfredo Stroessner overthrew dictator Frederíco Chávez.

Stroessner's Rise and Fall

Alfredo Stroessner and the Colorado party ran the Paraguayan government in the strictest tradition of the caudillos. The son of a German immigrant father and a Paraguayan mother, Stroessner was first elected to the presidency without opposition following an overthrow of the government by the military and police on July 11, 1954. He won eight consecutive elections with little opposition. Indeed, Stroessner allowed an opposition candidate to appear on Paraguay's election ballots only in 1963 and in 1988.

ECONOMIC DEVELOPMENT

In pursuing his country's development Stroessner carefully cultivated good relations with the governments of Argentina and Brazil, the two powerful nations with which Paraguay's economy is closely linked. Stroessner sought and received Brazilian financial support in the construction of the world's largest source of hydroelectric energy at Itaipu on the Alto Paraná River.

Stroessner also benefited from his strong friendship with the United States. The U.S. government helped construct the first all-weather road across the Chaco region, supplied experts to help modernize Paraguay's farms, and provided assistance to schools and public health facilities.

In providing effective local government, the Stroessner administration gave priority to Asunción—the area with the most people—with the intent of later extending services to less-populated areas. Thus, most development funds have benefited the more wealthy residents of the capital, while many of the nation's citizens remained without basic modern conveniences, such as plumbing and electricity.

Although Paraguay under Stroessner experienced economic growth, only a small group of wealthy Paraguayans benefited from the progress. Furthermore, the stability of Stroessner's long rule came at considerable cost to political rights and individual freedoms. Opponents of the regime were arrested, exiled, or murdered.

RECENT EVENTS

In the late 1980s, the elderly Stroessner began to leave day-to-day operations to his aides. But the question of the president's successor caused a split in the ruling Colorado party. This prompted General Andrés Rodríguez, second-in-command of the army after Stroessner, to take power in a violent coup in February 1989. Stroessner later went into exile in Brazil.

The fall of Stroessner brought demands for political reforms. Many legislators wanted the nation's leaders to become more independent of the military. In June 1992, a Constituent Assembly drew up a new Paraguayan constitution. The document confirmed the president as the nation's Commander-in-Chief, but barred General Rodríguez from running again for the presidency. The constitution also created a new post of vice president and expanded the Supreme Court from five to nine members.

At the same time, strong divisions were appearing within the Colorado Party. Traditionalists and a powerful military favored Stroessner's old policies, while their opponents favored new civilian leaders and further reforms. After bitterly contested party elections, the proreform Juan Carlos Wasmosy emerged as the Colorado party leader in March 1993.

In May 1993, Wasmosy won Paraguay's first free presidential election. A wealthy businessman, Wasmosy has moved to privatize (sell) many state-owned industries and open up Paraguay's economy to more foreign trade and investment. But his economic policies are strongly opposed by many members of the Colorado party, as well as workers who fear the loss of their jobs if the Paraguayan economy changes.

Independent Picture Service

From the Government Palace – whose architecture is modeled after the Louvre, a former royal residence in Paris – Paraguay's leaders have exercised power since the time of the War of the Triple Alliance.

Governmental Structure

Paraguay's new constitution establishes three independent branches of government —legislative, executive, and judiciary. The president and vice president, as well as legislators, are elected by a simple majority to five-year terms. All citizens over age 18—except police officers and those enlisted in the army—are eligible to vote.

The bicameral (two-house) legislature consists of a 45-member senate and a 80-member chamber of deputies. The senate writes laws concerning national defense and treaties, while the chamber of deputies has responsibility for legislation affecting departments and municipalities.

Paraguay's highest court is a supreme court, which is composed of a chief justice and eight associate justices, each appointed by the president to five-year terms. Special appeals courts decide criminal, civil, and labor cases, and civil courts handle commercial cases. Justices of the peace rule in minor cases. The country is divided into 17 administrative departments (provinces), each headed by an elected governor.

Residents of Asunción enjoy the refreshing waters of Lake Ypacaraí, about 10 miles east of the capital city.

3) The People

Paraguay can be divided into four major population groups, according to where the people live and how they earn their living. The Indians, who maintain their traditional lifestyle, reside in the Chaco and in the remote northeastern part of the country. Ranchers who live in southern Paraguay control huge estancias (estates). The eastern portion of the country is populated largely by European-born, commercial farmers, who have much in common with their kinspeople in nearby Uruguay, Brazil, and Argentina. In the central part of the country, along the Paraguay River and near Asunción, peasants and small-scale landholders farm the land.

Smaller groups include Mennonite settlements in the Chaco, Japanese agricultural colonies, and foreign groups in Asunción that manage industries, banks, and foreign trading firms. In all, approximately 4.8 million people live in Paraguay, and they are increasing their numbers at a rate of 2.7 percent annually—one of the world's highest population growth rates. Nearly half of the population is under 18 years of age. The current life expectancy is 67 years of age.

Spanish Heritage

Although Paraguayans are deeply proud of their Guarani heritage and actively promote its continuation, Paraguayan culture has been heavily shaped by its Spanish colonial past. Music, dance, religion, and customs all reveal Spanish influence. The system of social classes roughly follows the Spanish system, with nearly unbridgeable gaps separating rich from poor. In general, townspeople are considered to have higher status than country folk, and people who have been married in the church may look down on those whose matrimony has been a less formal affair.

Those who live in Asunción, in turn, think of themselves as better than those who live in smaller towns. And those in the capital who are of European descent enjoy a very comfortable standard of living. In Paraguay, two classes exist—"society," or those of means, and "people," or everyone else. Paraguay's oligarchy, or landowning and ruling class, is a small one—and one that is tightly knit through intermarriage and a common interest in preserving its wealth.

Peasant Farmers

Over half of Paraguay's people live on the land, but 42 percent of them are peasants who own less than 12 acres, and another 14 percent of them either own less than 2.5 acres or cultivate tracts they do not own at all. These landless farmers are squatters, or occupants of property to which they do not hold legal title. Some turn over a portion of their crop to a landowner who does hold title, and some pay the owner

Photo by Don Irish

Asunción's low-income population lives on the outskirts of the city along the Paraguay River.

Powerful oxen pull a plow to prepare a field for cotton planting on a farm near Santa Catalina, about 100 miles from Asunción.

rent for the use of the land. Others simply cultivate unused soil without any restrictions, working it until productivity declines —every two or three years. They then move on to another place where the earth has been unworked long enough to regain its fertility.

Peasants work long and hard at farming, using simple hand tools and ox-drawn plows. With such implements industrious families can grow enough food to live on. In rural areas, these laborers may have specialties besides farming. Men may work as herdsmen, plowmen, and carters (cart or truck drivers). They may saw logs, make charcoal, or engage in a handicraft such as making straw hats.

Some of the tasks associated with peasant life can be fun—like hunting carpinchos (water hogs), collecting wild honey, and catching wild parrots and monkeys to sell as pets. Monkeys that cannot be sold as pets sometimes serve a practical function: dressed up in red suits, they are

Harvesting sugarcane requires hard work and long hours spent swinging a machete, or long, heavy knife, such as the one held by the man on the left.

40

turned loose to frighten other monkeys away from the delights of raiding the crops.

Housing

The impermanence of the homes of Paraguay's peasant farmers matches the impermanence of their lives. Their houses are square structures made of adobe or of stakes bound together or plastered with mud—all with earth, clay, or brick floors, thatched roofs, and no conveniences of any kind. The mild climate is a boon to low-income Paraguayans, whose homes are often unheated.

Sparsely furnished, the rural home may include a couple of rawhide beds, a hammock or two, a low bench, a small table, and a wooden chest or box. In addition to these items, the average family's worldly possessions generally include basic kitchen utensils. Women often cook over a wood fire on the floor, the smoke escaping through chinks in the walls and roof.

Some houses are more elaborate, consisting of more than one room. Others have a tile roof. But even the most elaborate farm dwelling in Paraguay offers little more than shelter. In contrast, housing for the rich is much more spacious. Wealthy Paraguayans enjoy the comforts of heat, electricity, and indoor plumbing.

Courtesy of Mike R. Rassier

Rural Paraguayans prepare food in a cooking shed a short distance from the main dwelling. A three-legged grate on which a pot is placed surrounds a fire built on the floor.

Food

The diet of many Paraguayans is also simple. A common dish is a thick porridge made of dried beans, peas, or peanuts. The country's national dish is *sopa paraguaya*

Independent Picture Service

With walls made from local clay and reinforced by poles, this simple house is located on a farm in central Paraguay, near Villarrica.

41

Despite the fact that cattle raising is a major export industry in Paraguay, there still is not enough meat for everyone. In small town markets, beef is often sold out early in the day, and in the country it is available irregularly. Low-income groups seldom can afford beef, which they replace with cowpeas (black-eyed peas) for nourishment.

Courtesy of Mike R. Rassier

(Paraguay soup), a baked maize souffle. Occasionally, peasants are able to buy some beef at the local slaughterhouse or market. On the occasion when peasants grill beef or lamb over an open fire, everyone in the area is invited to share in the feast.

City dwellers eat a much more varied diet than country folk do, consisting of large amounts of meat—especially beef—and more vegetables. Meat is often prepared in a stew called *punchero* that is seasoned with onion, garlic, and vegetables.

The most popular beverage in Paraguay is yerba mate, a tea that men, women, and children sip out of hand-sized gourds through metal or wooden straws called bombillas. Taken frequently throughout the day, yerba mate tastes like alfalfa, and Paraguayans are as addicted to it as Brazilians are to coffee. Many rituals surround the use of mate. For example, when the mate bowl is passed around, to refuse a sip through the community bombilla is regarded as an insult.

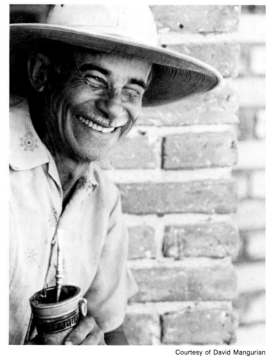

Courtesy of David Mangurian

This *tropero*—a cowboy of the Chaco—sips yerba mate, Paraguay's national drink, from a silver bombilla (straw).

Courtesy of David Mangurian

Many Paraguayan homes lack modern sanitation facilities. Here, women do the laundry in a local stream, spreading the clothes out to dry in the sun.

Women and Family Ties

Paraguayan women work very hard doing housework, grinding corn, cooking food, mending clothes, and taking care of their children. They also do the marketing and carry the water—tasks often requiring them to walk considerable distances. Despite the number of women's responsibilities,

men seldom help with such tasks. Women are limited in their job opportunities outside the home. They can be needleworkers, lacemakers, laundresses, cigar makers, small storekeepers, or cotton pickers to supplement family income.

In the Paraguayan family, as in lower-income families of Spain and Portugal,

Independent Picture Service

Three generations of women stand in front of their rural farmhouse surrounded by the children of a fourth generation.

marriage is likely to be an informal affair, with no church or civil ceremony. As a consequence, spouses may be changed frequently and easily. Marriages—in which loyalty is not strongly asked of either partner—often are dissolved, leaving the woman with the burden of raising the children. If the man or woman is unhappy, he or she simply moves out.

Religion and Festivals

While the Roman Catholic faith is important to Paraguayans, the people practice an everyday version of it that depends less on formal ritual than on cult worship of local saints. Paraguayans participate in religious societies that hold festivals on days reserved for honoring the patron saints of the societies.

Religious practices are broadened to include folklore—with respect paid to spirits like the *pombero* (who makes animal noises at night), the *pora* (the guardian of buried treasure), and the *yasi yatere* (who lures children into the deep woods when they are supposed to be napping). Paraguayans believe these Indian spirits must be won over if they are to be subdued.

At fiesta times, the Paraguayan polka is danced most of the night, and sopa paraguaya is likely to be served. Men usually drink *caña*, a fermented extract of sugarcane, though women will not openly partake of it. Since the drink is expensive and money is scarce, a man buying caña will pass the glass around to share a small sip with everyone present.

Education

The day may not be far off when Paraguay will achieve the goal of providing primary

In Asunción's Plaza Constitución stands the cathedral—a huge, square building flanked by two bell towers. Paraguay's coat of arms is displayed on the facade.

44

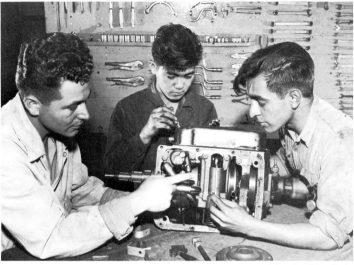

Though Paraguay has no auto industry of its own, the nation has a plentiful supply of trained mechanics, graduates of the Industrial Vocational School.

Independent Picture Service

schooling for every child. Progress toward this dream has been made in Asunción and in the principal towns, but in the country the obstacles are great, despite the fact that primary education is compulsory. An estimated 97 percent of Paraguayan children attend primary school. About 90 percent of the adult population can read and write, and the nation is proud that its primary school enrollment of more than 720,000 is increasing faster than the population as a whole.

By the time young people reach secondary school, they often must give up their studies to work in the fields to supplement family incomes. As a result, secondary enrollment is only 26 percent—much lower than primary enrollment. To persuade parents of the relevance of education, the government also offers technical and vocational education to young people. This kind of schooling has proved popular with both students and parents, the latter happy to have their children learn something practical.

Two universities offer higher education. The National University of Asunción enrolls more than 10,000 students, and the Catholic University, a private institution in Asunción, has about 7,000 students.

Wealthy Paraguayans, however, often send their children to universities in Argentina and Brazil for higher education.

Health Care

Hospital and health care are concentrated in Asunción, where over 70 percent of the

Independent Picture Service

The Paraguayan government emphasizes the teaching of technical skills. At the Industrial Vocational School, students learn how to repair radios.

Although Asunción is serviced by piped water, residents in much of the rest of the country rely on wells for their principal source of water. The World Health Organization (WHO) has aided Paraguay in its national campaign to clean up the sources of water — for example, by adding prefabricated, concrete linings to well walls.

A mother learns how to care for her two-day-old baby from a WHO technician. Rural Paraguayans commonly rely on folk cures that use herbal remedies. This mother, for example, wears a leaf on her forehead to cure her headache.

nation's doctors, dentists, and nurses practice. In contrast, rural areas have only about five doctors for every 10,000 people. Rural Paraguayans, when faced with a medical emergency, rush to the capital for treatment. Despite the lack of conveniently located medical services, Paraguay's infant mortality rate of 48 deaths for every 1,000 live births is relatively low compared to neighboring Bolivia's 75 per 1,000 or Peru's 81 per 1,000.

Many Paraguayans—both in the country and among the less wealthy Asunción residents—treat their maladies with a variety of folk cures. These include several herbs that have proved to contain beneficial qualities.

Art

As early as colonial times Paraguayans developed their own artistic style in painting and wood carving, a style called Hispano-Guaranian baroque. Although relatively few examples have survived, this artistic style employs decorative Guarani themes that are expressed in religious paintings and murals and on figurines. In the best of these, postures and facial expressions combine to communicate intense feeling.

Artistic output declined after the Jesuits were expelled in 1767. Although architecture saw a revival during the rule of Carlos Antonio López, it was not until the end of the nineteenth century that artistic expression enjoyed a permanent revival. Pablo Alborno and Juan Samudio established the National Academy of Fine Arts in Asunción in 1910. Alborno, who studied in Europe and introduced impressionism to Paraguay, specialized in murals but is also known for his landscapes and portraits. His best-known work is *Nanduti Lacemakers.*

Among Paraguay's younger artists Julián de la Herrería—a painter, etcher, and ceramist—is known for his sentimental depictions of Indians. Jaime Bestard's

In a painting entitled *Women of My Country,* Andrés Guevara offers a depressing social commentary on the hardships endured by those who live in poverty.

This wood engraving by Carlos Colombino is one in a series of pieces created in homage to Albrecht Dürer, a German artist who lived from 1471 to 1528. Colombino entitled this work *Tribute to Dürer* and modeled it after a Dürer self-portrait.

impressionist paintings portray fiestas, processions, cockfights, and landscapes. Carmen Fernández de Herrera—known as Laguardia—uses lacquer to paint religious and Guarani themes. Carlos Colombino paints on engraved wood.

Paraguay's most distinctive native handicraft is nanduti lace. *Nanduti* is the Guarani word for spiderweb, but the technique was probably brought to the New World from Spain. The intricately woven circular patterns depict common themes such as animals and flowers.

Music

Musical expression in Paraguay has been strongly influenced by the sad moods found in Guarani music. Native instru-

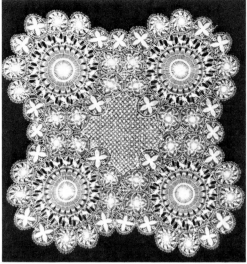

Independent Picture Service

Handmade nanduti lace, one of Paraguay's most intricate art forms, reflects Spanish and Flemish influences.

Independent Picture Service

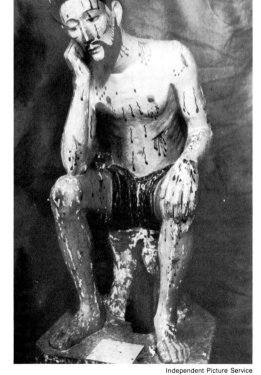

Independent Picture Service

These eighteenth-century wooden figures—*Saint Veronica* (left) and *The Agony of Christ* (right)—represent a style developed in the earliest days of European settlement.

Josefina Plá and José Parodi combined their artistry to create this modern, ceramic sculpture entitled *Native Rhythm.*

ments—which include vertical flutes made of sugarcane, wind and percussion instruments, rattles, bells, and gourds—are still used in remote areas. But the most

Where are you going, Josefa?, a ceramic plaque, was designed by Julián de la Herrería.

common instruments played today are Spanish guitars and harps.

Paraguay's most popular musical forms —the polka, the waltz, and the galop— all have been fused with native influences, taking on a slower and more somber air. Folk dances include the *Santa Fé,* which is similar to the Virginia Reel, and the *danza de la botella* (bottle dance) in which dancers balance a flower-filled bottle on their heads.

Literature

Most prominent among colonial Paraguayan writings are historical and legal studies, many of them written by authors who also have held important government positions. In the last years of the nineteenth century, Blas Garay produced four historical classics. In the most notable, *El Comunismo en las Misiones de Jesús,* he described the communistic system of the seventeenth- and eighteenth-century Jesuit missions. Juan Emilio O'Leary has written distinguished historical treatises on the War of the Triple Alliance in praise of Francisco Solano López.

Since colonial days almost all of Paraguay's writers have at one time or another expressed themselves in the Guarani language. Contemporary interest is reflected in poetic and dramatic writings in the native tongue that portray local social conditions. Modern writers of note include former president Juan Natalicio González, who has produced short stories and poetry of acclaim, and Justo Pastor Benítez, a former minister of foreign affairs.

Sports

Unrivaled as the most popular sport in Paraguay is *futbol* (soccer), which is played in every town, in fields, and at formal clubs. Asunción alone has about 30 clubs, organized into a competitive league. Clubs usually have their own fields, and some have seating accommodations for as many

Horses provide not only transportation but are also a form of recreation in Paraguay.

as 15,000 spectators. Local teams compete internationally with those from Brazil, Uruguay, and Argentina.

Basketball is the second most popular sport in Paraguay, and in 1969 the country won the South American men's championship. Paraguayans also enjoy hunting and fishing—which are done for both sport and food—in the country and on the principal rivers and tributaries. Horseback riding, a necessity on the ranches, has become a widely practiced pastime in the capital and major towns.

Netting fish is a business as well as a sport at the Tambo San Miguel fish farm near Coronel Oviedo. With seven ponds, the business has grown into an important enterprise where 50,000 carp and tilapia are raised.

Children grow up learning to swim at an early age in Paraguay, where the rivers and lakes are popular playgrounds.

To house the large work forces required in the construction of hydroelectric dams, the Paraguayan government has built completely new cities, such as this one at Yaciretá.

4) The Economy

During the 1980s, Paraguay enjoyed one of the highest rates of economic growth in the Western Hemisphere. Much of this activity was a result of international aid for the construction of roads and hydroelectric projects.

By the mid-1990s, however, the country's economy had been through several years of decline. A worldwide recession lowered demand for Paraguayan goods. Increased competition from neighboring countries also harmed Paraguay's inefficient firms. As exports stagnated, the nation's foreign debt increased. Unemploy-

ment and prices rose sharply. In addition, the government was losing money through public enterprises that it owned and operated.

Juan Carlos Wasmosy, who was elected president in 1993, took major steps to reform the Paraguayan economy. He planned to privatize many unprofitable public companies by selling them to private and foreign investors. By reducing social benefits, he also hoped to lower Paraguay's budget deficit.

Wasmosy and his advisers hope that these measures will eventually slow the rate of inflation and encourage more savings and investment. While reducing Paraguay's foreign debt, the government is also negotiating with international lending agencies for loans that will pay for further development.

These policies are similar to those being adopted in other Latin American nations. But many Paraguayan workers strongly oppose Wasmosy. Angry over falling wages, and fearing for their jobs in state-owned companies, laborers have demonstrated in Asunción and other cities. Wasmosy has also encountered opposition in the Paraguayan legislature.

Hydroelectric Power

During the 1960s, Paraguay built huge hydroelectric dams along the Alto Paraná River. Constructed jointly with Brazilian and Argentine funds, the dams doubled the value of Paraguay's total production of goods and services by the late 1980s.

These projects boosted Paraguay's economy by providing steady, long-term jobs for tens of thousands of workers. A whole range of related industries supplied the materials and equipment needed for dam construction. New towns created to house laborers and their families near the construction sites have stimulated the development of agricultural lands to feed the worker populations.

With the completion of the dams, Paraguay must now replace the thousands of construction jobs that have been lost. In coping with this situation, Paraguay is welcoming a steady flow of investment capital and technology from its neigh-

Courtesy of David Mangurian

The turbines at Itaipu Dam on the Alto Paraná River provide Paraguay with the world's largest single source of hydroelectric power. The nation began exporting hydroelectric power in 1969 through another project on the same river. Energy sales have become Paraguay's largest export.

Zebu, or brahma, cattle were orginally imported from India. Their resistance to local cattle parasites and diseases makes them well suited to Paraguay's warm climate.

bors, particularly Brazil. Brazilian entrepreneurs have recently made sizable investments in industry and agriculture.

Agriculture

Even with the new income from hydroelectric power, Paraguay continues to count on agriculture, its traditional economic mainstay. In 1991 farming and livestock raising accounted for one-quarter of Paraguay's gross national product and provided 90 percent of its earnings from exports. Agriculture still employs almost half of the country's work force.

All crops in Paraguay suffer from pest damage. Leaf-cutting ants pose the most serious threat to agriculture, but locusts, monkeys, and wild parrots also decrease crop volume. The cost of pest control is too high for most farmers, unless they belong to a cooperative. This farmer is able to purchase pesticide jointly with other members of his farming association.

53

Tobacco is often the first crop raised in newly cleared jungle. The jungle protects the soil from erosion by rain, leaving the land rich in nitrogen—a nutrient essential for tobacco cultivation. After a few years, rain washes away much of the nitrogen, and tobacco growing is no longer profitable. Tobacco requires special care at each phase of development. Seedbeds *(upper left)* are first prepared by treating the soil with insecticide and fungicide. Then seeds are covered with a thin layer of soil and are watered frequently. When the plants reach about six inches in height, they are transplanted—one by one—into fields *(upper right)*. By the end of the summer the leaves begin to yellow and turn thick and heavy, which means they are ready to harvest. The cut leaves are then carried to drying areas, bundled into bunches and hung over poles to dry in the sun *(lower right)*. Once the leaves are dry, they are compressed into bales and loaded onto trucks *(lower left)* that will carry the tobacco to market.

One of Paraguay's major cash crops, cotton is grown by many farmers. It is planted in September and October and harvested in February and March. Successful cultivation requires a long growing season with plenty of sunshine and water. Dry weather is necessary, however, at harvest time, so that the picked cotton can dry in the sun. Then it is baled *(right)* and loaded onto carts *(below)* to be transported to market.

Courtesy of Mike R. Rassier

Courtesy of Mike R. Rassier

Field workers take a break to relax and sip yerba mate, Paraguay's national drink.

Courtesy of Mike R. Rassier

Paraguay's principal cash crops are soybeans, cotton, sugar cane, corn, and wheat. Of these, soybeans have become the most valuable in recent years, because of increased demand worldwide for this product. In 1969 the country produced only 24,200 tons of soybeans, but by 1973 that figure had increased nearly sixfold, reaching a volume of 132,000 tons. In 1992 production had grown to 1.6 million tons.

Bad weather in recent years, poor-quality seeds, fertilizer shortages, and a lack of advanced farm technology have somewhat hampered the development of other cash crops such as cotton and tobacco. Farmers must deal with droughts, excessive rainfall, and periodic swarms of locusts.

Nonetheless, Paraguay's farms have continued to produce enough for domestic needs. Virtually every Paraguayan family raises maize and manioc (a fleshy root crop that is eaten like potatoes or ground into flour). In addition, plots of cowpeas, sweet potatoes, watermelons, onions, cabbages, lentils, peppers, lettuce, string beans, radishes, tomatoes, and carrots are also among the crops cultivated for home consumption.

Among the fruits that are commonly seen in the Paraguayan countryside are

Independent Picture Service

Manioc, a starchy root called *mandioca* in Spanish, preceded the arrival of the Spaniards and has long been a staple food in the Paraguayan diet.

grapes, oranges, bananas, lemons, coconuts, pineapples, cantaloupes, guavas (sweet, yellow fruits), avocados, mangoes (yellowish red fruits with firm skins), grapefruit, and apricots. As this list confirms, Paraguay can produce both temperate- and tropical-zone crops. This ability is a great advantage to Paraguay, since

Independent Picture Service

A farm worker (*left*) uses a machete to break up clods of earth. In rural areas, tedious, old-fashioned work methods are still in common use.

Near Pedro Juan Caballero, Japanese immigrants thresh rice on their farm. The Japanese farmers in this area also raise coffee, oranges, sugarcane, and wheat.

almost all of the food consumed locally is grown on the surrounding lands.

Besides supporting fruits, vegetables, and grains, the land is also suited to the raising of domestic animals. Only 2 percent of the country's land is suitable for raising crops. As a result, approximately 90 percent of all the farmland in use in the country is devoted to pastures, where a full range of animals—including dairy and beef cattle—graze.

SMALL FARMS

In the development of its land potential, Paraguay's most serious problem is that most of the nation's farms are too small to be economically self-sustaining. About 42 percent of all farms in the country are less than 12 acres in size, and 44 percent are between 12 and 48 acres. Such small farms, while they may produce enough to feed the families that work them, are not big enough to be competitive with the larger and more-mechanized farms of neighboring Brazil and Argentina.

Paraguayan farmers living on relatively small plots of land cannot afford, for example, to purchase tractors. In order to compete with agribusinesses in other nations, which are increasingly organized on a larger scale, the Paraguayan government has supported the formation of agricultural cooperatives. Through cooperatives, farmers can purchase jointly and can share the use of tractors and other equipment that would be too expensive for an individual farmer to buy. As this network of cooperatives becomes more effective, farmers will achieve savings through bulk purchases of fertilizers and seeds. They will also be able to market their crops on a scale large enough to earn maximum profits.

Some Paraguayans are resettling in the jungle near the Brazilian border in the northeast. These lands are more fertile than those in central Paraguay because they have not been over-worked. Clearing the jungle, however, requires long, hard work, slashing down the forests with a machete and then burning the stubble. Crops such as tobacco are then planted immediately in the remaining ashes.

RESETTLEMENT ON NEW LANDS

To increase agricultural productivity, the Paraguayan government is encouraging the resettlement of farm families on larger acreages that are potentially fertile but underdeveloped. Since 1960 the Rural Welfare Institute has helped to establish roughly 300 new farm colonies, some of them in areas where newly arrived immigrants from Europe had already begun to open up the land to cultivation. In the 1960s and 1970s, titles to some 2.5 million acres of public land were awarded to approximately 64,000 people willing to pioneer new farming areas of the nation.

The resettlement scheme is also helping to relieve land pressures in areas where too many farmers are concentrated on too little land—particularly in central Paraguay. To support the movement of people, the government has created several other agencies to assist farmers. The National Development Bank, for example, has increased the amount of credit for loans available to Paraguay's farmers. Special emphasis has been given to improving the nation's large tracts of pasture. Through breeding proj-ects the government also is seeking to upgrade the quality of Paraguay's herds of dairy and beef cattle.

Forestry and Manufacturing

The government has recently begun to ex-pand Paraguay's timber industry. At present, forestry employs about one-tenth of the nation's workers. Surveys indicate that Paraguay has more than 13 million acres of woodland with commercial potential. The government is trying to exploit this resource and yet conserve the forests for future generations. Forest products in-clude quebracho—from which tannin is extracted to tan hides—holly tree leaves for yerba maté, citrus trees, cedars, rub-ber trees, and coconut palms.

Paraguayan industry increased rapidly in the 1970s as a result of more foreign investment. But reduced investment during the 1980s hurt the nation's development. In the early 1990s most manufacturing plants were operating at about half of their total capacity. The principal manufactured products are food, beverages, and tobacco.

Workers load a cart with leaves from bitter orange trees, from which petit-grain oil is extracted. The fragrant, yellowish oil is used in perfumes, cosmetics, and soaps. Most of Paraguay's production of petitgrain oil is exported, and the country is one of the world's leading suppliers.

Courtesy of Mike R. Rassier

Independent Picture Service

These men harvest yerba mate leaves, from which Paraguay's most popular beverage is brewed. Until the twentieth century, yerba mate was gathered entirely in the wild. Now farm production has surpassed natural growth. Cultivated trees grow to about 30 feet in height, but wild trees grow much taller, which makes the leaves harder to collect.

Courtesy of Inter-American Development Bank

New roads are enabling Paraguay to exploit more of its huge forest resources. This sawmill is located in Ciudad del Este.

At a leather-tanning factory in Yaguarón, a worker presses an animal hide to soften the leather after it has been dried. An adjacent business makes work shoes.

Paraguay also produces textiles, clothing, leather goods, chemicals, paper and machinery.

In cooperation with Brazil, Paraguay's first steel plant began operation in 1986. In addition, an industrial estate has been developed for the town of Ciudad del Este, and a fertilizer plant has been planned for the department of Alto Paraná.

Transportation

Paraguay's level-to-rolling terrain has aided the improvement of the nation's highway system. The Pan-American Highway, running from Asunción east to the Brazilian border, is now entirely paved and carries an increasing volume of commerce. On the Brazilian side of the frontier, this paved route continues to Brazilian ports, so that Paraguay now has a reliable, all-weather land route to transport its products to the outside world.

The Pan-American Highway branches south toward Argentina as well, and that branch serves as another paved main artery for Paraguayan commerce. Daily bus service carries passengers to both Brazil and Argentina. For travelers with more time, a railroad runs southeast from Asunción to Encarnación, where a ferry crossing the Alto Paraná links up with the Argentine railroad system.

As road crews gradually expand the network of paved roads across the vast Gran Chaco region in the direction of Bolivia, pioneering families are following to open up and settle new lands for farming. Only

Paraguay is processing increasingly more of the food it grows on its farms. Workers at a plant in Asunción fill sacks with flour.

Courtesy of Mike R. Rassier

19 percent of Paraguay's roads had been paved by 1983. Since then, the nation has begun to pave more of its commercially important roads, which serve the eastern and most populous regions. Nearly 80 percent of all of the country's roads are located in this part of Paraguay.

More than a dozen international airlines service Silvio Pettirossi International Airport near Asunción. The busiest air routes from Asunción connect the capital to other major South American cities as well as to Madrid, Spain.

Foreign Markets

Until 1970 Paraguay's progress was severely hampered by shortages of electric

Courtesy of Mike R. Rassier

Cattle herds are frequently driven down the thoroughfares of Paraguay. Even the paved Trans-Chaco Highway across western Paraguay was built with especially wide shoulders to accommodate cattle herds.

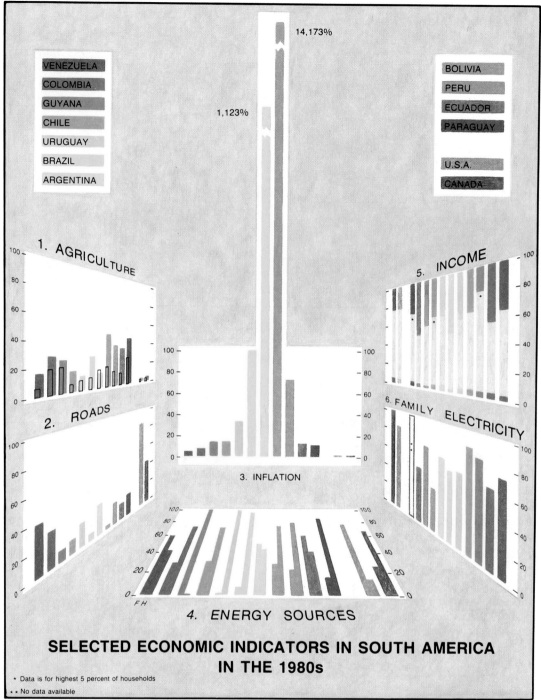

14,173%

VENEZUELA
COLOMBIA
GUYANA
CHILE
URUGUAY
BRAZIL
ARGENTINA

BOLIVIA
PERU
ECUADOR
PARAGUAY

U.S.A.
CANADA

1,123%

1. AGRICULTURE

2. ROADS

3. INFLATION

4. ENERGY SOURCES

5. INCOME

6. FAMILY ELECTRICITY

**SELECTED ECONOMIC INDICATORS IN SOUTH AMERICA
IN THE 1980s**

* Data is for highest 5 percent of households
** No data available

Artwork by Carol F. Barrett

This multigraph depicts six important South American economic factors. The same factors for the United States and Canada are included for comparison. Data is from *1986 Britannica Book of the Year, Encyclopedia of the Third World, Europa Yearbook,* and *Countries of the World and their Leaders, 1987.*

In GRAPH 1—labeled Agriculture—the colored bars show the percentage of a country's total labor force that works in agriculture. The overlaid black boxes show the percentage of a country's gross domestic product that comes from agriculture. In most cases—except Argentina —the number of agricultural workers far exceeds the amount of income produced by the farming industry.

GRAPH 2 depicts the percentage of paved roads, while GRAPH 3 illustrates the inflation rate. The inflation figures for Colombia, Guyana, and Brazil are estimated. GRAPH 4 depicts two aspects of energy usage. The left half of a country's bar is the percentage of energy from fossil fuel (oil or coal); the right half shows the percentage of energy from hydropower. In GRAPH 5, which depicts distribution of wealth, each country's bar represents 100 percent of its total income. The top section is the portion of income received by the richest 10 percent of the population. The bottom section is the portion received by the poorest 20 percent. GRAPH 6 represents the percentage of homes that have electricity.

The condition of Paraguay's roads reflects one of many hardships that a majority of the nation's people face daily. The government is gradually seeking to improve these conditions, however, so that more Paraguayans will enjoy modern conveniences.

power. The cost of generating power in the country used to be among the highest in Latin America, and per capita power consumption was very low. With financial assistance from international agencies such as the World Bank and the Inter-American Development Bank, Paraguay has dramatically increased its power output and has become a major exporter of power to nearby South American countries.

Besides power, Paraguay exports beef, soybeans, timber, cotton, and handicrafts to foreign markets. Foreign businesspeople, mainly from Argentina and Brazil, are increasingly active in Paraguayan commerce. European firms—some of them with branch offices in Brazil or Argentina—have also invested considerably in Paraguay.

In 1991, Paraguay joined with Argentina, Brazil, and Uruguay to form the Mercado Comun del Sur (Mercosur), a common trading market in southern South America. By joining Mercosur, these nations pledged to end all trade barriers among themselves by 1995.

The Future

The fall of General Stroessner in early 1989 also brought about the fall of dictatorship in Paraguay. During the early 1990s, the government dropped the harsh laws that Stroessner had enforced against those who opposed him and the Colorado party. The election of Juan Carlos Wasmosy in 1993 may well have marked the beginning of a new, democratic era in the history of Paraguay.

Having brought dictatorship to an end, Paraguayans are now facing serious economic problems, including inflation and unemployment. Although the new government is trying to encourage foreign investment, many Paraguayan industries are inefficient and unprofitable. More open trade among the South American nations is offering the nation a chance to prosper.

63

Index